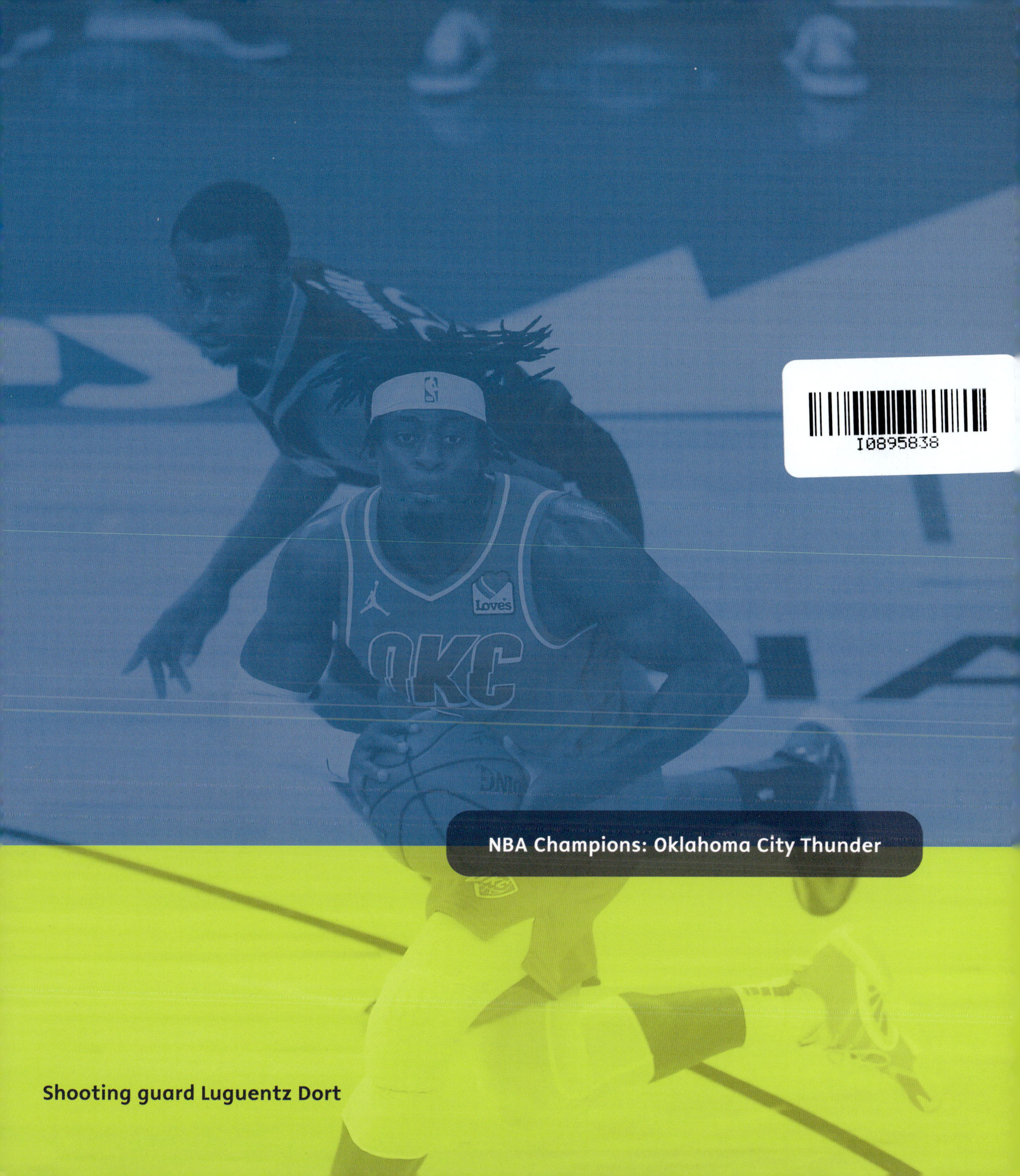

NBA Champions: Oklahoma City Thunder

Shooting guard Luguentz Dort

Guard James Harden

NBA CHAMPIONS

OKLAHOMA CITY THUNDER

JAMES BARRY

CREATIVE EDUCATION / CREATIVE PAPERBACKS

Guard Dennis Johnson

Published by Creative Education and Creative Paperbacks
P.O. Box 227, Mankato, Minnesota 56002
Creative Education and Creative Paperbacks are imprints of
The Creative Company
www.thecreativecompany.us

Art Direction by Tom Morgan
Book production by Graham Morgan
Edited by Grace Cain

Images by Dreamstime/ Jerry Coli, 19; Getty Images/ Dick Raphael, 12, Fernando Medina, 2, Focus On Sport, 4, 16, George Long/WireImage, 15, Jared Wickerham, 7, Jeremy Woodhouse, 9, Joshua Gateley, 10, Patrick Smith, 24, Larry W. Smith, 5, Layne Murdoch, 3, Rocky Widner, cover, 1, Ron Hoskins, 6, Sam Hodde, cover, Sean Gardner, 20

Library of Congress Cataloging-in-Publication Data
Names: Barry, James (Author of children's books) author.
Title: Oklahoma City Thunder / by James Barry.
Description: Mankato, MN : Creative Education and Creative Paperbacks, [2025] | Series: Creative sports. NBA champions | Includes index. | Audience: Ages 7-10 | Audience: Grades 2-3 | Summary: "Elementary-level text and dynamic sports photos highlight the NBA championship win of the Oklahoma City Thunder, plus sensational players associated with the professional basketball team such as Shai Gilgeous-Alexander"—Provided by publisher.
Identifiers: LCCN 2024018494 (print) | LCCN 2024018495 (ebook) | ISBN 9798889892625 (library binding) | ISBN 9781682776285 (paperback) | ISBN 9798889893738 (ebook)
Subjects: LCSH: Oklahoma City Thunder (Basketball team)—Juvenile literature.
Classification: LCC GV885.52.O37 B37 2025 (print) | LCC GV885.52.O37 (ebook) | DDC 796.3230976638—dc23/eng/20240502
LC record available at https://lccn.loc.gov/2024018494
LC ebook record available at https://lccn.loc.gov/2024018495

Printed in China

Guard Russell Westbrook

Forward Jeff Green

CONTENTS

Home of the Thunder

Oklahoma City is a fast-growing city in the southern state of Oklahoma. It is sometimes called OKC. One busy place in OKC is an **arena** called the Paycom Center. A basketball team called the Thunder plays there.

Point guard Shai Gilgeous-Alexander

The Thunder are part of the National Basketball Association (NBA). They play in the Northwest Division. That's part of the Western Conference. Two of their **rivals** are the Minnesota Timberwolves and the San Antonio Spurs. All NBA teams want to win the **NBA Finals** and become champions.

Forward Spencer Haywood

Naming the Thunder

The team started playing in 1967 in Seattle, Washington. They were called the SuperSonics then. People often called them the Sonics. A vote was held to pick a new name when the team moved to OKC. Most fans chose "Thunder." Oklahoma gets many powerful thunderstorms. The Oklahoma-based 45th Infantry Division was also known as the "Thunderbird" Division.

Thunder History

One of the Sonics' best players was guard Lenny Wilkens. He played and coached in Seattle at the same time for three seasons.

In 1978, the Sonics reached the NBA Finals. They lost to the Washington Bullets. The next year, Seattle faced Washington in the Finals again. Great guards Gus Williams and Dennis Johnson helped the Sonics stop the Bullets. The Sonics were champions!

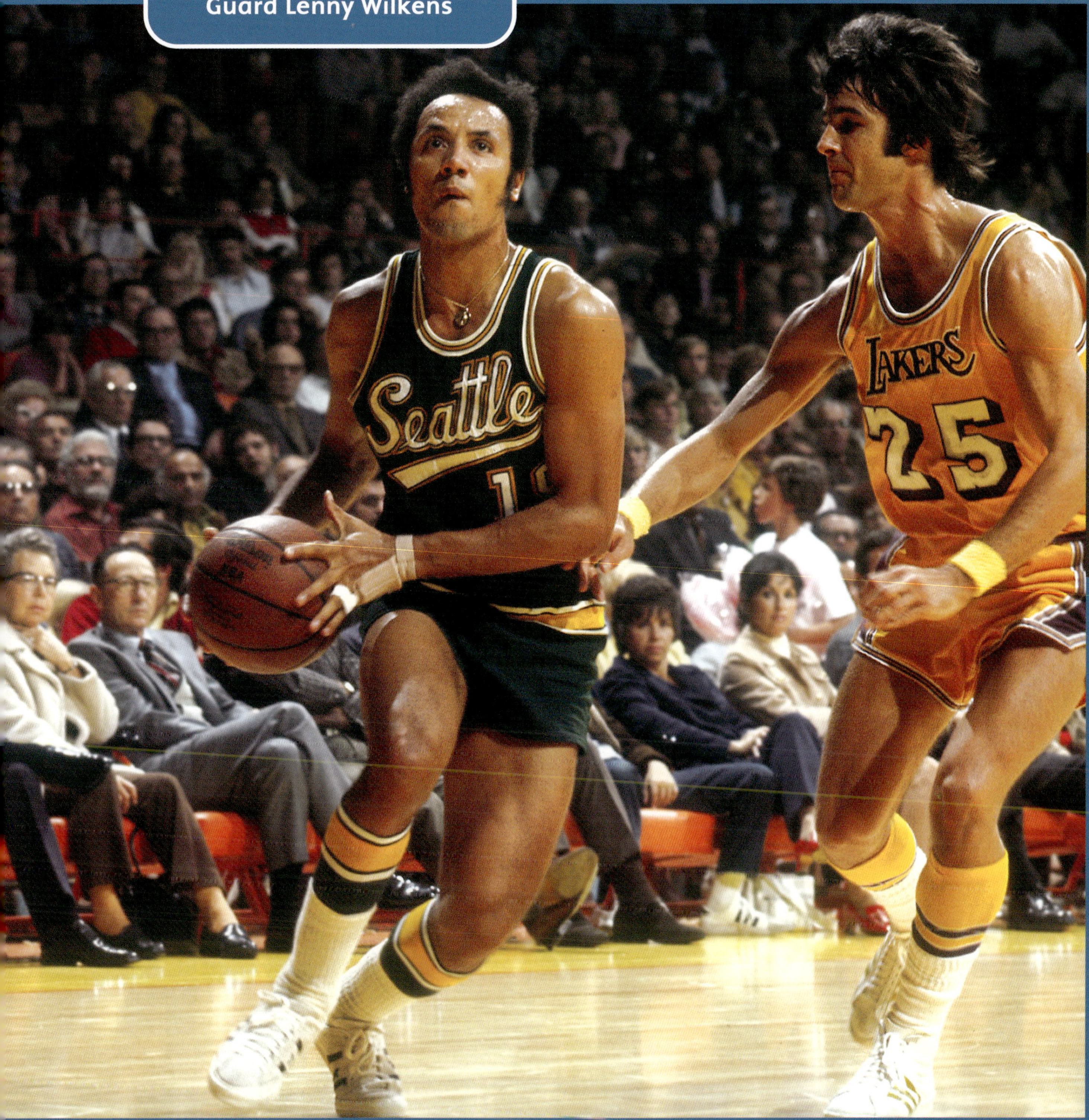

Guard Lenny Wilkens

Forward Shawn Kemp

The Sonics made it to the 1996 Finals. They lost to the Chicago Bulls. Their fans still loved to watch powerful forward Shawn Kemp slam the ball through the hoop. They also cheered for tough point guard Gary Payton. He was named the NBA's best **defender**.

In 2008, the Sonics moved to Oklahoma City. They became the Thunder. New fans in Oklahoma cheered for high-scoring forward Kevin Durant. He led the team to the 2012 Finals, but they lost to the Miami Heat.

Other Thunder Stars

The Thunder have had many other great stars. Center Jack Sikma was a strong **rebounder**. He was a big part of the 1979 championship team. **Versatile** guard Nate McMillan was called "Mr. Sonic." He played in Seattle for 12 seasons. He later became the team's head coach for five years.

Center Jack Sikma

Guard Russell Westbrook

Fierce guard Russell Westbrook had an amazing 2016–17 season. He won the **Most Valuable Player (MVP)** award. He set records with his scoring, passing, and rebounding.

Tricky point guard Shai Gilgeous-Alexander joined the Thunder in 2019. He became an **all-star** a few years later. Thunder fans hope he will soon lead OKC to an NBA Championship!

About the Thunder

First season: 1967–68

Conference/division: Western Conference, Northwest Division

Team colors: Thunder blue, sunset, navy blue, and yellow

Home arena: Paycom Center

NBA CHAMPIONSHIPS:

1979, 4 games to 1 over Washington Bullets

TEAM WEBSITE:

https://www.nba.com/thunder/

Glossary

all-star—a player picked to play in the All-Star Game, featuring the season's top stars

arena—a large building with seats for spectators, where sports games and entertainment events are held

defender—a player who stops the other team from scoring

Most Valuable Player (MVP)—an honor given to the season's best player

NBA Finals —a series of games between two teams at the end of the playoffs; the first team to win four games is the champion

rebounder—a player who catches and controls the ball after a missed shot

rival—a team that plays extra hard against another team

versatile—able to do many different things well

Guard Josh Giddey

Index